0

Forex Trading

Effective Strategies & Tips to Build your Wealth in Forex Market

ALI KHAMIS

Table of Contents

Book Description

Have you been thinking of building your wealth lately? Are you thinking of buying that dream house? Do you wish to travel the world to all the places that you have always dreamt of? Well, Forex trading is the way to go! Getting started on Forex trading requires a little bit of educating yourself. One of the attitudes that you will have to put on is to approach it like you would any career, because trust me, that is what it is!

To develop your trading skills, you need a Demo trading account. One of the biggest mistakes that most people make is going into forex trading like they do a lottery. You need to be ready for you to make it worth your while. A demo account will allow you to trade for a while so that you can fully understand the strategies that are available and the manner in which the market works. In this book, we will be discussing some of the most effective forex trading strategies that will guarantee your success. We will also dig deeper into some of the best money management strategies and tips.

Many traders lose money trading forex because they are inexperienced and they neglect these forex management principles, you do not want to be one of them. What you have to understand is that the forex market is high risk-high returns strategy mainly because of its volatility. It is therefore a non-negotiable success factor that you can leverage as a beginner.

With this book, you will gain insight into the best ways in which you can manage your trading capital when trading forex. You should not just aim to make profits from a single trade, rather, it is important that you base your strategy on making profits over a very long time. This is exactly the point at which managing finances and trading capital is vital, and you do not want to miss that. So, what are you waiting for? Let's learn all things forex trading and build our wealth!

Introduction

Did you know that maintaining your discipline is one of the critical factors when it comes to forex trading? While this is important, one of the things that you have to understand is the manner in which you can enforce that discipline when trading forex. One of the ways in which you can achieve this is having a trading strategy that you can stick to. The best strategy is one that has been well-thought out and back-tested. This is what gives you the confidence that you are using a strategy that will guarantee your success. It is that very confidence that will ensure that it is easier to adhere to the rules of trading-maintaining discipline.

Often, when people discuss Forex trading strategies, they are referring to a specific trading method that unfortunately, is one facet of a complete plan. For your trading strategy to be consistent, it has to provide advantageous entry signals that are important in position sizing, risk management and how to exit the trade eventually.

One thing that you have to bear in mind is that the most profitable forex trading strategies vary and do not necessarily have a definite answer to it. The main reason for this is that best forex trading strategies are suited to the individual trading. This simply means that you have to consider what your personality is and then use the information available to you to work out what the best strategy is for you. In other words, what may work for me may not necessarily mean that it will work for you or someone else?

On the other hand, a strategy that is often discounted by people may even turn out to the best one for you. Therefore, if you are going to achieve success trading forex, you have to be ready to experiment a lot. It is by trial and error that you will be able to eliminate all those that will not work out for you and I will show you how. One key aspect that you have to remember is having a definite timeframe for your trading strategy.

So, what is forex trading really?

The place where currencies are traded is often referred to as forex exchange market. The truth is, currencies are very important to people all around the world, whether they know it or not. This is mainly because you need to change currencies for you to conduct a foreign trade and business. For instance, if you are living in the UK and would like to buy cheese from France, you will make payments for the cheese in euros (EUR). This simply means that the UK importer will have to exchange the equivalent of Sterling pounds (£) into euros. This is exactly what happens also when people are travelling to different countries.

The need to exchange currencies is the principle reason why the forex market is considered the largest and the most liquified market across the globe. It is the very thing that dwarfs other markets with respect to size. in the US alone, an average of $2,000 billion is traded every day in Forex exchange. There is no central market place for Forex exchange and this is what makes it quite unique in the international front.

Trading often happens over the counter. This simply means that all transactions happen via a computer network that connects the traders all around the world. This is opposed to a one centralized exchange. This market is open 24/5 ½ days every week. The currencies are traded worldwide through the major financial centers that include; Sydney, New York, Hong Kong, London, Frankfurt, Singapore, Zurich and Paris among others. This simply means that when trading day comes to the end in the US, it only begins in Hong Kong and Tokyo among others. As such, forex trading is something that stays active anytime of the day and night and is characterized by constant change in price quotes.

How institutions trade Forex

There are three major ways in which most financial institutions trade Forex. These ways include; spot markets, futures markets and Forwards market. Forex trading in the spot market is one of the largest markets across the entire world. This is mainly because of its underlying real assets that the forwards and the futures markets are based. Over the past decades, the futures market was considered the most popular place for most FX traders, mainly because it was available to most individual investors.

However, since the advent of electronic trading and the many emerging forex brokers, the spot market has taken the limelight because unlike any other, it has witnessed a surge in activity. Today, it has surpassed the futures market and is currently considered as the preferred trading market for individual investors as well as many people who are speculating. Therefore, when people talk about the forex market, they are simply referring to spot market. On the other hand, the futures and the forwards market are less common with investors but are popular with most companies that require to hedge the risks

11

associated with foreign exchange out to a specific date in the future.

Spot Market

To be very specific, one thing that you have to appreciate is that the spot market is the place where currencies are bought and sold based on the prevailing market prices/value. That prevailing price is often determined by such factors as demand and supply. It therefore, is the reflection of quite a number of things that include; economic performance, interest rates, political situations both locally and internationally. It also reflects perceptions about future performances of one currency as compared to another.

Once the deal is complete, it is referred to as the spot deal. In other words, it is the bilateral transaction through which one party delivers a currency amount that they agreed upon with their counter party so that they can receive a specified amount of different currency at an exchange rate value that they agreed upon. Once the position is finalized and closed, the settlement is done in cash. Despite the fact that s the spot market is often said to deal with transactions in the present, the trading only takes about 2 days to reach settlement.

Forward and Futures Markets

Unlike the spot market, the futures and the forwards markets do not deal with trading actual currencies. Rather, they simply deal in contracts that often serve as claim representation to a certain currency type. They also have a specific price per unit as well as a future date for the settlement. One thing that you have to bear in mind is that forwards market involves contracts being purchased and sold over the counter between two contracting parties. These parties are responsible for determining the terms of their agreement.

On the contrary, the futures markets, the contracts are purchased and sold on the basis of a standard size as well as the date of settlement on public commodities markets like Mercantile Exchange. In the United States, it is the responsibility of the National Futures Association to regulate it. The contracts in this case have a specific date and minimum price increments that are not customizable. In other words, it is the exchange that serves as a counterpart to the trader, offering settlements and clearance.

Both the forwards and the futures contracts are legally binding and are mainly settled for cash for the exchange concerned once it expires. However, one important thing is that you can still buy or sell before the contracts expire. Both the futures and the forwards markets have the capability of offering protection against a wide range of risks when trading currencies. In most cases, you will realize that international corporations leverage these markets so that they can hedge against rate fluctuations in future exchanges.

Forex trading styles

There are several types of trading styles that range from short time frames to long time frames. These methods have been used widely over the previous years to date. The good thing is, as you continue to grow into a fine forex trader, your skillset becomes more refined and you will be aware of the different trading styles and strategies available in the market and hence determine which one works best for you to achieve forex success. These styles include;

Scalping

This is often a short-lived trading approach that you possibly hold for just but a few minutes. In this case, the scalper often seeks to beat the offer spread as fast as they can while skimming a few points of profits before they are closed. Scalping uses tick charts similar to those used by the MetaTrader 4 supreme edition, which offers some of the best forex indicators for tailored for this approach.

Day trading

These simply refer to trades that are exited before the close of business each day. This often gets rid of the chance of being affected by large moves that often occur during the night. This strategy is usually one of the best forex trading approaches especially for beginners. In this case, trades often last a few hours and the price bars on the charts may be set typically between a minute or two. 50-pips is one of the day forex strategies.

Positional trading

This is often a long-term kind of trading strategy whose main aim is to maximize their profits from the major price shifts. This is suited for long-term traders who pay a close attention to the end of day charts. Some of the best positional trading strategies needs the traders to exercise immense discipline and patience. Additionally, if you are going to use this strategy to trade forex, you have to ensure that you have adequate knowledge of the market fundamentals.

Swing trading

This is a trading strategy that is held for several days. In this case, the main aim of the trader is to make profits using short-term patterns in pricing. In other words, the swing trader might look at the bars every few 30 minutes to an hour to determine a patter and sure it to make successfully accurate predictions.

Why trade forex?

Forex is one of the largest markets in the world with over $4 trillion traded each day. It is this exceptional liquidity that plays a significant role in ensuring that the pricing is reliable even when volumes are high. This also ensures that the tightest possible deals are equitably spread. Therefore, when you trade forex, your trading costs are lower and you have potential of going short or long of any given currency.

In other words, when trading, you will always be going short on one currency and long on the other. This is mainly because you are exchanging one currency value for another. It is this that in reality offer you the opportunity to make profits from the relative weakness of a given currency or the weakness of another currency.

Considering the fact that forex is traded across the world, there is a possibility of taking a position for 24 hours a day throughout the trading period in the week. However, you have to understand that currency values are extremely sensitive to the forces of macro-economics, meaning that trading opportunities are always present.

How to choose your forex broker

The key requirements to having a trading broker are because of the low trading costs and the effortless execution. There are so many trading brokers that are available in the market. The InterTrader for instance offers you no dealing desk betting spread on both its major and minor forex pairs. They also offer 100% neutral execution in the market.

You could also choose to use MT4, which is a web-based platform that offers you forex trading opportunities where you can trade a wide range of indices, equities as well as commodities among others. All these you can trade on the same account. With these platforms you will get access to;

Free trading tools: that include those that play a critical role in forex analysis, live squawk as well as technical research.

Spread betting: which allows you to the select a forex trading vehicle that suits your needs, goals and ambitions.

Fractional pip pricing: the main aim of this is to ensure that you quote forex to an extra decimal place so that your profits are sharper.

Live webinars: so that you can learn a few tricks when it comes to trading. It also includes archived webinars which will help in determining the patters and strategies used over time and help you project where training will position itself in the future.

Forex Trading Signal

As a forex trader just like the others out there in the market, you could benefit from some accurate trading signals to use. A trading signal simply refers to a bunch of indicators of when and how to trade certain forex pairs on the basis of a specific price analysis. In most cases, these trading signals may be generated from a manual source as well as an analytical program that utilizes complex technical indicators/signals.

One thing that you have to bear in mind is that you have to be methodical when using trading signals. The best way to achieving this is by simply finding clear and reliable trading sources that you can recommend on the basis of methodology. This methodology has to also be consistent with a wide range of trading strategies. The good thing is that, most signal providers supply the research that underpins recommendations from individuals while also offering accurate details on the strike rate using previous signals as a baseline. There are two major trading signals; entry point and the exit point.

Trading signal: entry point

It is the entry point that tells you what the price level is hence determining the level at which you can open a trade on the forex pairs of your interest. It could be that you want to buy the pairs hence a long-position; or that you want to sell the pairs hence a short position. Typically, you have to understand that the entry point is set at a particular level that in turn triggers a large market activity, based on the analysis that underlies the signal.

For instance, with Inter Trader, it is possible for you to create an order that is aimed at opening a new forex position. This is especially the case if the price hits a level that is already predetermined. This simply means that you do not have to be active on your end once the entry point is breached.

Also, you could choose to set a price alert at the entry point so that you can manually open a trade once that alert is triggered.

Trading signals: exit point

With a reliable trading signal, you will typically get two exit points. These exit points indicate the point at which you can close any positions that were created in response to a signal. This simply refers to the stop level and take profit level, otherwise referred to as the limit level.

It is the role of the stop level to tell you where to close the position especially in case the trading is moving adversely with the aim of limiting possible losses. On the other hand, the role of the limit level is to tell you where to close the position especially if the trade is progressing favorably so that you can lock in your profits.

For example, a signal may indicate a rise in the short-term price which is then preceded by a reversal. In such a case, you will need to take your profits at the peak before the profits are reversed. Both the stop and the limit levels are very critical when it comes to designing a successful trading plan. They also are very important in helping you define what your personal risks and reward systems are as well as helping you stick to the levels that you have defined instead of running your profits or chasing after your losses.

InterTrader for instance allows you as a trader to set your stop and limit levels for every trade that you make. Once these levels are triggered, the position will be automatically closed. One thing that you have to remember here is that the stop orders are not guaranteed, hence, they may be subject to slippage and market gaps.

Tips to Build your Wealth in Forex Market

The steps to managing your forex money management and building your wealth include the following;

Quantifying your risk capital

The first thing is for you to calculate the risk associated with the trading process. If the chances of making a profit is lower as compared to profit gains, you had better stop trading. The best way to determine this accurately is by use of a trading calculator so that you can effectively measure the risks. Understand that most of the important aspects of building wealth and managing your forex money beings with this value.

For instance, the size of the risk capital serves as the determining factor of the upper limits of the position size. Therefore, it might be prudent to put no more than 2% capital at risk in any trade. In addition to this, you can always ensure that you implement risk management in every trading strategy that you use so that risk management is effective.

Avoid trading too aggressively

One of the biggest mistakes that most new traders make is trading too aggressively. In as much as we know that high risks are often associated with high returns, it is important that you take this with a pinch of salt. This is mainly because, if s small sequence of losses is adequate to eliminate most of the risk capital, it simply means that each trade is associated with too much unnecessary risks.

One good way to target or focus on the best risk level is making adjustments to the position size so that it gives a true reflection of the volatility of the forex pairs you intend to trade. However, you have to remember that the higher the volatility of the currency demands on a smaller position, the lesser the volatility of the forex pairs.

Admit it when you are wrong

Run your profits and cut back on loses, is the golden rule of trading. This simply means that you have to exit as fast as you can whenever you have clear evidence that you have made a bad trade. The truth is, you are human and it is natural to try to turn a bad situation into a good one. However, in forex trading, this is a mistake. The main reason for this is simple-you cannot control the market forces.

Make use of stop losses

One of the good things in using stop-losses is the fact that it will help you initiate good money management, hence contributing to building wealth. In other words, it is the stop loss that plays a critical role in protecting all your investments as far as unanticipated market shifts are concerned. Considering the fact that there will always be a possibility of making a loss, it is better if you set your stop-loss order below 2% of your trading balance for each trade that you make. For instance, if you have a trading balance of $10,000, your recommended stop-loss should be estimated at around 40 pips per trade. This means that, if the trade does not go the way you expected it to, all you lose at your stop loss should be $40.

In forex, there are so many types of stops. However, the manner in which you place your stop loss depends on your personality and level of experience. Some of the most common types of stops include but is not limited to; equity stops, chart stops, volatility stops and margin stops.

It is important that you understand that a good money management approach when it comes to forex trading is survival. Survival is the highest priority. This means that, profits will come after and should not be at the forefront. Start by preventing losses and you can achieve this easily by using stop-loss processes. The point is for you to ultimately accumulate your profits. If you realize that you are always making losses, take a step back and analyze your stops to determine to transform them into something useful.

It might be time for you to make adjustments to your levels so that you can begin to reap better trading outcomes. Stop-losses are very essential in helping you cut back on losses and they are even more beneficial if you are able to monitor the market more effectively. At the very least, if you do not want to use an actual order in the market, you should try using a mental stop. You could also make use of price alerts, email alerts as well as text alerts especially with such plugins as MetaTrader 4 Supreme Edition.

Be very realistic

The reason many traders are overly aggressive when it comes to taking risks in trading is because they have unrealistic expectations. For most traders, having that aggressive thinking is thought to help them make profits more quickly. But the truth is, this is not realistic. The secret is for you to try as much as you can to make steady returns on investments. When you set realistic goals, you maintain a conservative approach, hence making trading a success.

Do not trade on the tilt

In forex trading, you may suffer a bad loss at some point. You may also burn a large portion of your risk capital. One thing is that so many people are often tempted to get their investments back within the next trade once they make such big losses. However, here is the problem; increasing your risks when your risk capital has been lost is the worst thing to do at this point.

Instead of taking such a move, it is better if you consider reducing your trading size in a losing streak. You could also find it useful if you took a break until you are able to identify a trade with a high chance of winning. The point is, stay on an even keel both in terms of position sizes as well as emotionally.

Always be ready for the worse

Don't get me wrong, past performances are not necessarily indicative of the future outcomes. The truth is, when it comes to forex trading, we cannot really know the future of a market. However, we have so much evidence from the past. What has already happened in the past may not repeat itself but is important in showing what is possible. Therefore, always ensure that you look at the history of the forex pairs that you are trading. Think critically about the actions that you need to take in order to protect yourself from making losses that might have happened in the past.

In the process, it is important that you do not underestimate chances of price shocks occurring. In that case, you need to have a plan B for when such a scenario happens. It is not necessary for you to dig deeper into the past to find examples, but you can find those that made a huge impact.

Envisage some exit points prior to getting into a position

On the upside, what are some of the levels that you are aiming for? What level of loss do you consider sensible for you to withstand on the downside? Determining these two major factors plays a significant role in helping you maintain your discipline when trading heats up. It also will serve as an encouragement when you begin to think of it in terms of risks versus rewards.

Respect leverages and understand them well

The good thing with a leverage is that it offers you an opportunity to boost your profits that you derive from risk capital that you have available. It also increases your potential for risk. In as much as this is a very powerful tool when it comes to building wealth in forex trading, it is essential that you understand the size of the whole exposure. The truth is, your broker may give you some leverage so that you can make profits but you have to be very careful when using the platform.

For instance; if you have a leverage of about 1:100 on an account of $400, it simply means that you can place a trade for up to $40,000. On the contrary, applying a leverage of 1:300 means that you trade up to $120,000. In other words, your exposure level is increases with increase in leverage.

Therefore, if you are just starting off in forex trading as a beginner, it is advisable to avoid higher leverages. You would be better considering a leverage once you have a deeper insight on the potential losses associated with it. This way, you will not suffer major losses and hence stick to the right side of the market. All things kept constant, leverage is still an advantage of the forex market. This is because it can help you make more but it can also make you lose more, hence trade with caution.

Different leverages are offered by a wide range of admiral markets based on the results of the trader. Ion such a market, traders are often classified into two broad categories; professional traders and retail traders. In such markets, the leverage often is set at 1:30 for retail traders and 1:500 for professional traders. In both classes, there are wide range of benefits that you can enjoy and you can always talk to your broker to find out what is available to you.

Have a bigger picture that spans into the long-term

One thing that stands to reason is the fact that success and failure in trading can only be determined by the long-term performance. Therefore, it is important that you stay alert when it comes to apportioning great importance to success and failure of your trade. Do not ignore rules or try to bend them in order to make your current trade work, it might just be the biggest mistake that you make. Always stick to the rules and see the bigger picture.

Advanced money management tips for forex traders

One common problem with most forex traders is the ability to money their money. If you are going to build wealth from forex trading, then money management should be your number one skill. You have to have some tips and tricks that will help you make the whole difference. For you to be successful, these tips will come in handy in helping you become even more successful in trading. All these tips will require you to be disciplined in the trading process by adhering to specifically set rules. Once you have mastered these tips, you can implement them and see how that effectively builds your wealth.

Do you have a forex trading plan?

If you do not already have one, then it is high time that you have it and stick to it no matter what. It is in this plan that you have effective money management strategies. With a trading plan in place, you will not only be able to keep your emotions in check but also will help prevent you from over indulging in the trading process.

When you have a plan, your entry and exit strategies are well defined. This simply means that you know when to take gain, cut losses as well as avoiding greed. In other words, it is the one thing that will help bring discipline into your trading plan, something that is critical for you to successfully manage your forex capital.

Avoid greed

It is quite tempting to want to make supernormal profits within the shortest time possible. It is this greed that has the potential of leading you astray to making the worst mistakes and trading decisions ever. You have to realize that trading is not about opening the right trades at the right time and then terminating them if they were wrong. It is about maintaining discipline and sticking to the strategy that suits you. This is the only way you will be in a better position to boosting your trading potential.

Have protective stops

In the previous sections, we have discussed deeply what stop-losses are. However, one other important factor is the use of protective stops in forex trading for effective money management. Protective stops are a form of stop-losses that often results in profits. In other words, once you have a position and have a floating profit of about $500, it is important that you set a stop-loss that would yield a floating profit of about $100 based on the chart. This way, though the prices fluctuate drastically causing you to hit your stop-loss, you will still reap some profit.

Covering capital losses

During the process of trading and money management, the process of covering capital loss is quite challenging. For instance, if you lose $2,000 by simply investing $10,000, the percentage loss is 20%. In order to cover this loss, it is important that you make a 25% profit with the same amount. It is important that you pay a close attention the commissions and spreads offered, as this is a potential expense. Ensure that you are able to cover all these expenses and the costs that you incur so that they do not end up making a huge negative impact on your entire life.

Above all, do not stress over the trading process. Always be comfortable with the amount that you are willing to invest and everything else will go smooth because you will not beat yourself over it.

Conclusion

The information that we have presented here will help you get started in forex trading. It will simply lead you towards a well-structured approach to trading so that you end up becoming a refined trader. Just remember that, trading is an art, the best way to boost your proficiency is through consistent trading, sticking to the strategy and the rules of the game as well as practicing discipline. Everything else will definitely fall into place. Happy trading!

Done!